A SUITABLE LOVE OBJECT

A Suitable Love Object

REBECCA SWIFT

Valley Press

First published in 2020 by Valley Press
Woodend, The Crescent, Scarborough, YO11 2PW
www.valleypressuk.com

First edition, first printing (September 2020)

ISBN 978-1-912436-44-6
Cat. no. VP0164

A CIP record for this book is available from the British Library.

Cover design by Matthew Young.
Text design and additional editing by Jamie McGarry.

Printed and bound in Great Britain by
TJ Books Limited, Padstow, Cornwall.

Contents

Foreword

Many of us remember Becky bursting into song – she preferred public places, parks under various bird calls, or European museums where the echoes appealed to her – and she always insisted that you join in. Even now she is still a wonder to me; there always existed the wild possibilities of laughter in her conversations.

More privately, there was her deep and loving knowledge of the poetry of Emily Dickinson, as evidenced in her biography of the poet, *Dickinson: Poetic Lives*. And, even more privately, there were Becky's own poems, which she wrote for most of her life. Reading these now, you discover the intimate Rebecca who had that wild sense of humour, but also sadness and a tragic sense that was always with her, too. The poems she wrote were tender, excessively private, and so often to do with loss:

> When you are secret with me and I've
> least idea of where you are, you are
> silent as the blueness of the vein
> running still beneath the skin.

Nearly every one of the poems in this book has wonders in it. Many delight in tales of family politics, or describe the narrator falling in love – poems which are joyous as well as sad, yet always full of grace such as 'The End of Things' or 'Grandfather – and Cat'. But most are heartbreaking, even if they may end with the escaping tone of seeming whimsy which is, however, still loss, as in the poem 'Comparison':

> I entrust my soul now to the shrivel mouse.
> What happened to us –
> when the fire ran in and ate our house?

Michael Ondaatje
2019

Introduction

Soon after Becky Swift and I became friends – in what would turn out to be, improbably and tragically, the last decade of her life – I decided she was one of those people it was possible to know very well after only a short time. In part, this was because of the warmth of her manner, which didn't allow for dawdling in that region between acquaintance and friend; once Becky decided she liked me and I indicated the same, we very quickly moved into friendship proper. But this was also because Becky could be so unfiltered in conversation, particularly about herself, sharing intimacies and conversations that went right to the heart of things.

So, over the years, as we walked through Hampstead Heath in all weather, Becky leading the way in her endearingly bossy way that came from her love for – and therefore feeling of ownership towards – the Heath, she would talk about her life, its sorrows and its joys, and the influences that shaped her. I knew that her love for literature came from her mother, Margaret Drabble, and her love for music from her father, Clive Swift. I knew about people she'd lost, in one way or another, over the years and how that cost her. I knew about her periods of clinical depression; knew about her interest in the link between writing and therapy; knew how much satisfaction she took in the continuing success and growth of TLC (The Literary Consultancy), the organisation she co-founded and ran, which provided professional editorial advice to writers working at all levels; knew the happiness that she found with her partner Helen Cosis Brown; knew probably more about her circle of friends than they would have wanted a stranger to know. Though when some of those friends and I came together around Becky in her last months when she was fighting off cancer, they didn't feel like strangers at all.

What I didn't know about for a long time was Becky and poetry. It was probably quite early on that she mentioned she wrote, or had written, poetry, but it was always in a manner that was almost a side-note. She certainly didn't attach the title 'poet' to herself. Mostly in those first few years when she talked poetry, it was with reference to Emily Dickinson, whose work she loved, and whom she was writing about for Hesperus Press' *Poetic Lives* series. Occasionally she might reveal that some of her poems had been anthologised, but it was always a subject she moved quickly on from – I made the mistake of thinking perhaps poetry was merely something in which she dabbled.

Then in 2014 during an exchange of emails, when I was complaining about something I had to write, Becky mentioned she'd just written a poem about Doris Lessing, who she'd known since she was a child, and who had died just a few months earlier. 'Send it!' I said, and something about email's immediacy convinced her to do so. 'Hope it makes sense. It sticks to the required form anyway,' she wrote, in characteristic fashion.

The required form was a sestina, one of the most difficult of forms to convincingly stick to. From the first haunting line, I knew that my assumptions about Becky and poetry were untrue: 'There's a place where the dead meet and the dogs get lost.' The poem was beautiful, wry, brimming with intelligence and insight and love – the sensibility behind it was very much the Becky I knew, and at the same time there was something new in it that made me see that I had been wrong to think my friend so easily knowable. Here, in the demanding form of the sestina, I saw her from a new angle.

Why didn't Becky publish more in her lifetime? I was wondering about precisely this question when it struck me that I might find an answer in her Emily Dickinson biography. I started reading, and in the introduction came to this sternly-worded sentence: 'It is best to make clear at the outset that Emily Dickinson will remain a mystery'. Very well, Becky, least mysterious of friends – have it that way. It is perhaps enough to know that, unlike Dickinson, she didn't leave behind a secret cache of poems with no instructions about what – if anything – she wanted done with them. Becky was putting together some of her poems in a manuscript with a view to publishing, and *A Suitable Love Object* is that dream brought to fruition, as she instructed, by her partner

Helen Cosis Brown and her beloved friend Melanie Silgardo.

The title poem, in thirteen parts, is clearly about the therapeutic experience; it opens with the startling lines: 'Because you understand that my love might not be love / but something terrible, even clawed and ill / [...] I am free to love you.' It moves through different registers of grief, anger, contemplation, disdain – there's even a reference to a musical thrown in that raises a smile — but most of all there is an honesty, tensile strength and control of language that moves through the sections to quite extraordinary effect.

Elsewhere, there is the playfulness that was so much a part of Becky's character, as in 'Sudden Meditation on Form': 'On a train I read a modern sonnet / and wonder what the force and full effect of rhyme? / Does free verse have a sting in bee and bonnet / or does poetry that meanders stray in time?'

For the most part, though, playfulness was what Becky did out in the world; her poems were largely a place to look both at darkness and the light that pierces through it. In 'Down' she writes of understanding the pull towards suicide. 'Again, again / I see it – / there it is – / a hollow tube. / I see from here to there, / me here – / death there –' and a little while later, the unexpected piercing note of elegy: 'Yet don't I recall better times, / when the green lands lit by evening suns / were reason enough?'

But more often when death stalks these poems it is in the form of those Becky has loved, or loves, and whose loss is so hard to bear – even before they're lost. Anyone reading the villanelle 'Practising of Ghosts' might find within it an embedded reference to Becky's love for Elizabeth Bishop's 'One Art', but it isn't a poem that leans on any other as its rhymes and refrains circle the idea of trying to prepare for further loss in the wake of loss: 'You who have not died, lend me your pre-imagined ghost / to prepare the art of losing'. If that poem could be said to have a companion in the collection it is 'Doppelgänger Friend': 'And now we're walking, my doppelgänger friend and I, / now we're climbing, sitting, gazing at the sky. / How much more time we spend together / now you terrifyingly are not here.'

It is still sometimes unimaginable that Becky is, terrifyingly, not here. But how glorious to have this collection to spend more time with her for those who knew her, and to discover her for those who didn't have the chance. The final poem 'Where is it We Go?' is one I won't quote here; it is best to come to it in the right order, at the end of the journey through Rebecca Swift's beautiful mind. I'll say only that it feels like an act of great generosity from her towards everyone who reads the poems to know that in the end, what she most wanted was to stay among us.

Kamila Shamsie
2019

After Wordsworth

There is nothing on earth so beautiful
even now, though the poet's dead and gone
this glittering view once looked upon;
the river glides, strong and slow and full
and Parliament histories the scene,
yet more than gentle Wordsworth saw has burst
along the banks since London's edge was green.
St Paul's, once undisputed King's now dwarfed
by Gherkin, New Rose, Blade and Oxo Tower;
the water is bedecked, bedazzled and bewharfed
a blossoming of late commercial power.
Who knows the future? Will the once-brief Millennial Eye
still round us, hound us, and outstand us, when we die?

Driftwood

Mankind struggles to build a permanence everywhere
Attachment decoys the void
One truth resounds
By necessity as much as by wisdom
Human love is incomplete

Let go
Let go
Let go

Getting Rid of Things

First, a crutch
Then a shower cap
Then the edges of love

A whisky bottle you chose
A book you'll never read
A shirt
Then, slowly, hope

A broken egg
A wooden bird
Whose symbols you abandoned
Overrode

These things slowly
One by one
With varying degrees of pain
Sometimes none
I discard
Into plastic bin

Dull enough to bury all life in

You, Most Beautiful of Women

You, most beautiful of women;
because you are perennially absent
and have become a ghost in grey
and tweed, who sits and waits for me
with death-like patience on street corners
this pointless evening in chill September.
Your silver, lungish presence
could be done with tonight
for a quick drink after work; a quiet
game of cards at your house
in a room I have never seen
somewhere familial; somewhere you and I could
swim together, gently, unalarmed.

How far could we let each other wander,
when I have allowed you to breathe for me
and you accepted to breathe?

In Memory of Doris Lessing Walking on the Heath

There's a place where the dead meet and the dogs get lost;
where four roads meet, by willows and strip-green, catch-eye
    parakeets,
which some call bastard foreigners;
you were a migrant too; left violence far behind,
for 'political innocence' and table-talk;
you left your children too, but one said she 'didn't mind'.

The one who clung had died, but the others 'didn't mind',
she said so at the funeral, in the same church where the dead get
    lost.
(Dreams now, they seem, spider, plumber, space, and table-talk;
childhood memories rare and florid as the strip-green, catch-eye
    parakeets.)
You left two children far behind,
some called you violent foreigners…

You thought of us, you said, one homely meal, as foreigners,
'Political innocents' in England, soft-padded of the mind –
'You have no idea.' Communism gave you a son, and left some
    far behind.
(Some thought your mind, and then your son got lost.)
Now when I hear the shriek of catch-eye parakeets
I recall the treasured 'gone-wrong' son, and treasured table-talk.

My mother's house fuelled table-talk,
and though you thought of us as naïve foreigners,
(odd as strip-green, catch-eye parakeets)
you invited yourself in, and mother didn't mind –
the Heath on which the dogs got lost
was close, and none then left behind.

When you travelled into space, you left most far behind
(you spared us this at table-talk) –
you took off to where the world gets lost,
and humans all are foreigners –
you'd left Rhodesia, then this planet-earth, but your daughter
    understood; she said at church, she didn't mind
(though others thought you alien as strip-green, catch-eye
    parakeets).

Then with mental-flight, strange as Heath and willow parakeets,
your Sufi whirling rendered you, or us, behind,
but pudding-bound we laughed and drank, we loved and didn't
    mind.
Ah Doris, now you're gone we miss your table-talk –
you and your special son both now spectral foreigners,
I found your ghosts where the dead meet, and the dogs get lost.

It was at the place where the dead meet, and the dogs get lost
where ghosts, like spectral friends, not foreigners,
sang to me this poem, and said you wouldn't mind.

Sestina – for Melanie Silgardo

Mind Cull

I would cull my mind for you
Lay at your feet the kill
Stag, beaver, butterfly, each last
Mosquito-meshing light-on-the-hill
Every nuance of sunset
I would bring to you—
Only there is too much over-spill
Our time is short
My mind itself in over-kill

I know you would if you could (Buddha-like)
I know you would if you could (magic-wand)
I know you would if you could (contain-the-world)

But we are subject to large laws
Like the cracking up of dinosaurs

Practising of Ghosts

You, who have not died, lend me your pre-imagined ghost
to prepare the art of losing; up the memory-laden hill
I practise with your spirit: whom I loved most.

You, who have not died, lend me your pre-imagined ghost
obeying your not-long-to-be everlasting will
I practise with your spirit: you, who loved me most.

The suddenness of birds is living beauty's boast,
sun-struck cliché round the wood – the chill;
somewhere ahead is the violence of the coast.

Two died that left no time for practice, no time to toast.
So now, with terror and with thrill
I practise with your spirit, habituate your ghost:
I never will be parted, from those that I love most.

Grandfather – and Cat

There was a pitchless whistle designed for
dogs (he got it anyway), this, silver
like a promise we could not hear and then
a hiatus – a nothing – a green horizon
and from several acres away over
perennials, shrubs, Christmas trees, that anchorless lawn
you tilled, the ridiculous bound of him,
Maximilius, fat, white cat, more tended,
more wanted, more fed with rich meals in
bowls on more sacred ground he walked on
than anything else, it seemed, and now seems.

Golf clubs stand darkly, idly, behind the
front door, bashed silver and gold
like the weight of small hearts.
You saying Keats was the best and the worst
('Tiptoe up the Little Hill' – but listen to
'The Nightingale') of verse.
There were leather-bound books from
second-hand shops: Shelley and Beowulf too;
a novel called Scawsby, by you: mnemonic, play havoc.
Now, in theme of you (yes) –
somewhere this cat-white foam in this impromptu bath
reminds me of Max – and of you.

Upon Remembering Getting into Bed
with Grandparents

It's amazing we got that far, loveless
as you were supposed to be, yet suddenly
I have a longing for your tripeish thigh;
swallows, thronging to the eves; a teasmaid
playing boring Sunday news and all sorts of
rites and rituals which seemed notable but
were really just trips in and out of the
bathroom, the neurotic pulling back of
curtains, stained glass window at the top of
hall stairs; dark chocolate like the secret
meaning of the world in a corner cupboard:
three-quarter circle smooth as a child's
dreams and as far above reach...
'Loveless', the daughters said, years later when
the slow-lack peppered in their brains like a dust
and life had grown troublesome as thought.
But just tonight I am thinking of your thigh
and of the unconscious swallows thronging to the eaves.

Auntie Phyll

With your life curled on your knees just under
your breast, white and curly-fluffy, named
Daisy, you sit, all cream-tea and chops;
all orchard with real pears and apples
bitter to taste unless cooked up; all
pantry with musty nothing in it; all
Peter the canary, who ate yellow-headed
groundsel; all paddock with
God-knows-whose donkey in it; all
local school with a tropical tank, all
gawp at little sharkey, black-bodied
red-tailed vibrant, strange fish;
outlandish, to be so bold.

Once I sat upon a boiling spa which

Once I sat upon a boiling spa which
bubbled up, irregularly, and still it
bubbles up, I do not understand it, totally,
but now, you know, I can speak of love
and hope – because you converse in such language
openly – you make it true (truth you know, takes two).
Now, entering into something new, I feel
despair, yeah, sure, I've felt it before
too often – far – for it to vanish now, the
undesirable miracle which will not last, because it
is not real. You know normally, I could not utter
'hope' without a backlash into fear; 'love' without a
retrogressive sneer I could not control – and even now I
feel the spear – you know… but even so,
you allow me to be free: not necessarily to
recreate the patterns – doomed to stifle me.

The End of Things

September came heavily, heralding the
end of things; you, for example
and the bitter apples on the tree
we collected loyally but which sat in
paper bags endlessly until decay
loved them more than we ever could.
September fell heavily, monsoons in
Haringey, torrents over tiny bridges
sprouting madly, unsound roofs let
water in (I noticed, oddly, now that we're
selling the garden with the apple tree).
Winter grew heavily; and as sharp days
darkened, we negotiated an ending
quietly in curtained-again rooms;
your thick drape threatened terribly to
hold me and make me feel warm –
whilst quickly now, no longer wanted apples
fell from trees and rotted silently in the uncut grass.

Depressive Position

I had a shoal of dreams
to scatter me with means;
might mean, meant.
In streets I lose my way
baffled by the day,
head debates and feeling wronged,
righted, blighted by concern for
love of you. This will not do.
Something deep is over, massacred
forever, fairy tales of you –
also don't come true.

In dreams I find the sadness
strange and sad – but true –
but in my head you'll wear my scarf forever
in blue, and ordinary blue.

Golden Girl

The Golden Girl sang gold
until the twist;
addicted to golden moments
she broke the wrist
of a best friend
trying to be first to catch the dawn.

Trying to be first to catch the dawn
she felt
something sudden, soft and sharp
beneath her sulky feet
and looking down
a secret slug lay torn.

Golden girl knelt down
(to reap the secret slug
which squelched out underfoot),
she held it high
examined it and saw
the magic core she'd known before.

Golden girl stretched up
to see the sun,
she thrust her arm
and arched her back,
she cricked her neck – and saw
the sun was black.

A Finnish Affair

An utterly still lake with
utterly lifeless pines
surrounding it like soldiers
guarding always against nothing.
A curlew which does not fly,
cranes which form no formation,
a boat which holds dreamy you and I
alighted by the midnight's gloomy sun;
barely, even, betrayal…
Lilies, magic-leathery
negotiate the liquid black
like little Christs,
claustrophobic and cool, cool, cool
against the uncertain deep.

A Saxophone Plays by a New Grave

A saxophone plays by a new grave,
gold as the inscription. A light rain falls.
Gangs of friends, some younger and more dissolute
than others, blend and bind here around you.
A weak sun offers a thirsty light and we seek for
rainbows, urgently, amid alien stones.
We feel unfamiliar in this marked garden,
have not had cause to visit here often.
It was not expected, such violence from you;
you, who could not bear to kill a fish
nor even hear talk of such a thing.

Weekend Walk in Porlock

A half moon on my left.
A split sky just ahead.
A white flower come from
nowhere in my hand;
a snailish brain
unfurled to glare
at an even, evening sea
loving rocks into sand.

I impressed you without you knowing

I impressed you without you knowing
and lost you when you knew

and hunger for possession cuts
dignity in two

and exposed the child and fool in me
I destroyed in my confusion
that insane illusion of worth
where of course there is none
that a child or bird has not.

I humbly, humbly leave you
but with a prayer or two
that blindness is shed, the moment regained
through surrender, my dear,
of you.

If

If in your darkness
you fall far
into the back of
that mind –

back far, where lurk
demons and mountains
of black
and fear

where, lost
an emptiness fills you
and shrouds you –
and silver dullness

stretches for years
beyond and around
and you can see no seed
from which

your essence grows,
and to which it clings,
with pain so blue
and clear –

remember that, although
your life seems cold,
and creativity old –
or dead;

the flame is warm.

Lovely Ladies

There are so many ladies now I cannot
see for the thick of them nor
tell anymore who is who is who.
All have swapped clothes in dreams so
many times that I'm
blown if I know anymore who is who is who.
It's melted somewhat into a
motherly glue, yet still, still
for all those lovely ladies, all their love
I cannot make my stories true.

Counterbalance

I always wanted you, counterbalance. Counterpane.
I always needed you to drain the silt from the
underside of love, to cater for the excess of the above.
I need you to be the small brown bin into which I can cast it –
the pain (that stupid noun again).
The 'this doesn't belong here now';
temper ill-rising, mid-afternoon, for no reason.

I want you to filter away, with love, the
bad syntax in sentences, those moments
out of sync, the curious panic,
rising up at irregular intervals caused
by the mere turn of the head. The wrong word. A sentence
too long, or too overspoken, or too overheard.

I want to fill my bucket up and meet it.
Yes. Put on protective clothing. Fish it out and
beat it – without a stick – just by
somehow knowing it,
letting it out into the garden
and hanging it up at last
up on the clear white line for the
acerbic sun to blast.

A Suitable Love Object

Because you understand that my love might not be love
but something terrible, even clawed and ill;
because you understand that my love will probably not be love
    at all
but something else, something which may want to kill you;
because you understand that my love cannot really be love
because it is too much mixed with all
sorts of things, like memory, and the self
and what imagination has offered up to me,
I am free to love you
and every thought becomes a match to
illumine unexpected caves which
whisper deeper understandings of you.

2

There was no such thing as leaving.
Life quietly arranged a death, a wedding, a selling-up
and broke me open,
sleepless, weakness,
made me thin again.

It's you and I
bi-weekly
with our holding and our dreams;
who now would be rid of whom?
What would it, that room,
look like, now, without our
furnishing?
The final statue, maybe
in a bonded row of three?

3

Funereal you feel, poised like a shade at the
end of my day; all our meetings are fare-thee-
wells, which once flared up like the fantastic
findings-out of love; yet still, I must come.
Oh Mistress of the Almost-hour, my time is near.
Free, almost, to enjoy the ordinariness of being
alone; to catch a sad bus in the rain, to go shopping,
to worry about the bills and the washing-up;
fail to do what I now even fail to imagine to do.
How dutiful you have made me; I could not now
refuse these last Visitations though the
terror may do me good. Like a good girl now,
at last, I end, I end into nothing.

Oh dark Saint, oh dark Routine; with my first
free act, as well you know, neither of us shall
delight my leaving: I shall just go. I shall
just go, onto the 29 bus in Camden Town
into the round-about-me-now-everywhere snow.

4

'Love me,' she said, 'you are allowed to
love me – I want to harbour all your love
to examine it most closely.' And so we
swam together, inside that little room.

My senses thrived my brain outcried until the
pipe sounded like a boom, I could not permit it;
it sounded as drums from a foreign tribe and you
concurred and risked 'it's weird' and for that
hour, the 'harbouring' began to work its charm –
but I began to fear the life outside that little room.

5

When you are secret with me and I've
least idea of where you are, you are
silent as the blueness of the vein
running still beneath the skin. You are
magic as the gold at core of microcosmic
flowers, you are the tremendous
buzzard, with tortoise shell wings,
clicked free from the great tree by my
passing, quite off the beaten track.

6

Only the snow can articulate this
separation, and it does so, succinctly
to my beleaguered feet which twist now, quick
as sun-fall, into part-objects twenty
humiliating yards from your door. Only
you require that a moment of your time
is worth more than sanity, and with this
consideration, you freeze me, thaw me.

7

Because now, all other loves are built on you;
because you have become this wild fountain
without which there is no home, no love,
I call you a deity almost
and obey the winds and rains of you.

I am bound to good opinion of you
as we are bound to love the air;
the calculating winds
which put us here.

8

The intermittent almost-hours decreed and
squared affection like an old master. Love
spilt from the conversation like a milk and
begged to be taken seriously, but there was
nothing in the contract that was happy
with this. Salt recoiled up mothering ducts
and peculiar thoughts sprang up like wild flowers,
scattered, by the unaccountable mouths of birds.

9

Love spilt around the edges of the conversation
like a milk, while the intermittent almost-hours
contained affection like a hearse that bore them
backwards, as far as minds can go; then
everything left, and somebody smarted like a snake
by a long-abandoned pit it hadn't reckoned on.

When all is said and done
you're just another 'funny' face
(but you – at quite a price).
I like you anyway – for what it's worth,
usually. I do not see you at parties
crumbling peanuts awkwardly –
drinking or abstaining (both would anger me).
I do not see your temper frayed
slightly too late at the end of the day.
I do not see you when the love you have is spent,
when you are not quite at home,
when you have to speak out alone,
when I would have to criticise you seriously,
away from these four walls, and me…

What kind of affirmation is it you receive?
Day in, day out, with the cripples at your knees?

The game is up, Mrs Muck.
Why don't you call your husband back?
The magic's gone. You've been exposed.
My mind is closed to you.
Now you can throw me out
at three, or four, or five.
I come for you out of a
vague sense of politeness. Nostalgia.
A harping back. I suppose
you played your part. Now
go smear your muddied face over another,
another angling heart.

She will never throw you back up to me.
She is the sea – the drowning sea
whose naked roar's 'reality',
but you were more than that to me,
than life-denying fantasy.
(She thinks I cannot see?)

Though now you seem all chimera
or narcissistic mirror –
my once so well-beloved –
the horror – oh the horror.

I would disappoint you if I loved you.
I would become like all the rest,
lounging with their feet up,
just wanting you to give up
so much you would become useless to them.

But you know I am not so cool: I love you
secret as the blueness of the vein flowing
still beneath the skin; hidden as the
great birds sudden-flap their wings from
off-beat trees;
as much as I know you would imbibe these things
if not for your sake, then for mine,
because you are made that way
for whatever locket-reasons
you will never let me know.

John: Picture

You say you've been standing
where the coral combed the sea
and you say that that black mountain's
all there will ever be.

You tell me you've been seeing
waterfalls which do not flow,
you tell me you've been painting
trees, like bombs, which backwards grow.

You climbed a hill, found cave paintings,
spear heads, four and
spaceman's trail, gold mines,
iron mines and fridges,
sixty-eight in number, free,
all cascading down the mountain
as they made their way to me;
hissing, sighing, moaning, crying,
old asbestos slowly dying,
flowing from the coal-dry sea.

You tell me that you watched the ocean
as the sun set in the west,
just behind a pearl boat's motion
(gently rocking, as is best)
and as you watched two cranes flew over
(or so the traveller's story goes)
and as you looked up, waters shook –
two giant turtles rose –

Wind Song

The wind is testing everything
in this great and sudden inquisition.
It's asking:
how much can we take
of the storm within?

It's become a kind of torture.
The sun's a naked bulb
in the sky, made fierce by something as
small and pointless as an aerosol can,

and instead of calm after the storm
there's wind upon wind and more wind.
A new wind. Wind without storm.

The wind is scarring everything
in this cruel, ungentle ultimatum.
It's asking:
how much can we take
of the burning within?

It's become a kind of trial of air.
The sky's a hangman's mask
in a world made blue by something as
insubstantial as strange smoke up there.

The wind's confronting everything
in this wild, unsubtle occupation.
It's asking:
how much can we take
of the manoeuvres within?

It's become a kind of battleground.
The earth's a worn-out patch
in a land made square by something as
trite and as tragic as the struggle for a piece of ground.

The wind's upsetting everything
in this cold and sad investigation.
It's asking:
how much can we take
of the deluge within?

It's become a kind of overflow.
The rivers are rich tears
crying down to unmagical seas
fed by unnatural mouths.

Fragment

A poem does no harm.
It does not pin
crime to crime nor charm to charm,
rather it wanders in the spacey regions,

is happy with a fragment
for maybe only that was meant.

Sudden Meditation on Form

On a train I read a modern sonnet
and wonder, what the force and full effect of rhyme?
Does free verse have a sting in bee and bonnet
or does poetry that meanders stray in time?
I like the result of calculation –
that said, there are things I prefer:
a tough errant application,
a break – a pause – a blank – defer
all of meaning until out of form it pours,
obeying strangely, like a mirror, nature's ruptured and vesuvian laws.

The Urn

You fled to the limit of my projections
then finally, out of sight,

until I could no longer say I knew you
nor be clear if I ever had.

When we met you were Athene.
You said the gods had thrown away the mould;
you said so yourself
and I, laughingly, agreed.

It was fun then,
this self-mythologising.

Just now I thought of you
as some figure on a Grecian Urn.
Now you're fled and horribly gone;
some strange mythical woman
who loved and loving split herself open
then ran, ran, ran
away from all love's expectation

out, out, away
into, it seems, another person's play.

Down

Again, again
I see it –
there it is –
a hollow tube.
I see from here to there,
me here –
death there –
and the dullness,
the black,
the beauty,
whirling and unfolding…

Who would desire to undergo
the trial of spinning lunacy,
when he can shoot,
without touching the sides,
unscraped
into the inevitable?

Yet don't I recall better times,
when the green lands lit by evening suns
were reason enough?

So are we so helpless,
as to need await an indifferent sun?
Or is each of us a blind master
of every colour the mind sees
and, frightened,
leaves?

Doppelgänger Friend

In memory of Kate Hill (1965-1994)

Since it happened, we spend
longer together than we did, and at
odd moments of the day, too.

Last night, for example, you dropped in at, say
four or five a.m. – healthy, welcome, warm and
altogether bemused when I railed at you,
fanatic: 'Go back. Get out. You're dead.'

I'm sorry, I don't know what came over me.
But there you were again at breakfast;
quieter, calmer, altogether more benign,
joining me for tea, privy to my latest thoughts about John Major,
how I thought I might spend my day.

And now we're walking, my doppelgänger friend and I.
Now we're climbing, sitting, gazing at the sky.

How much more time we spend together
now you terrifyingly are not here.
Just three short months
into this, our first insubstantial year.

Last year my mind was in a dustbin

Last year my mind was in a dustbin.
Recovery was written off.

I hurled – how I hurled
into space towards no thing,

but now, on a dull January morning
plodding back to work

I want to tear the walls down,
fling open windows.

I want the lighter air on my nose,
the tang-white air in the trees.

Wonder of wonder.
Miracles of miracles.

This ordinary human –
this all-too-common thing.

My heart leaps towards the spring.
My fresh-aired brain craves everything.

Comparison

My soul is in jeopardy
with the shrivel mouse.
Every time I walk into her house
I long for an enabling love
– like we used to have.

But it is always the same;
the name she speaks
is not my name.

I entrust my soul now to the shrivel mouse.
What happened to us –
when the fire ran in and ate our house?

Reverie

These things do I see:
a bird, a blue,
the green of an olive tree.
We two are always just in love.
You are the flash of dove
flying low above the flood,
crying always,
silently.
The world will be at peace now,
emblematically.

It happened as I always knew it would

It happened as I always knew it would.
Poised in a gallery, a Russian Cameo
so stuffed with beauty, just at the exact
moment when Passion had answered its long-
nurtured question. Love, though, sang a
different tune and hung between us
like a moon, unclear if it has anything
to do with the earth or not.

Pagan Soul

I knew you had a pagan soul when I
first saw you in your long coat, striding a
giant's stride at dusk, that
dark and green November;
silver-pacing through willows and through
mud as if it loved you and you hated it.

Wet-foot and angry, with your fashionless
uneven hair that some called ugly, some mad,
but the best knew as vision, you were a poet –
a wild and wordless prophet. That turn of your dear
head that sought and fought the low geese,
for all their beauty's pain,

was the very soul's poetry. Though your words are
lost now, drawn from your eyes alone
that night; they are drowned in coal-black ponds.
Dead forever to all but I who
caught all that night in the turn of your
head.

I care for the mad, for the poor and the weak, and
weep for the tramp with his cold and his drink yet I
lie. Nothing, I care for nothing but the soul, and yearn for
nothing but a sense of well-meshed soul. We wager our
love on some sense of sense that may be true or may not –
if not, then we are as nothing as is integrity

and that greying sky. We dedicate ourselves to flame and live to
master it, but it splutters and rages distinct from us
sometimes: and that is why I love, more than anything I love,
I love you at the lake that night, for I have wagered my
life on the turn of your lost
head.

Meanderings

WATERING
(ANNAFFIARE L'ORTO)

Hot and bothered,
the watering is done –

when the wet hits the flowers
the fragrance comes –

the cracked earth rejoins and swells…

When the wet hits the flowers
the fragrance comes.

CARNIVORES

The chickens spied the earwigs
whilst I was heaving hay –
I never saw such a massacre.

TONI

Toni – like a watermelon in her
striped-green dress –
rolls round, over, after dinner
and thinks of names for the children…

The Geese and the Wind

1

The geese stood
upright against the wind –
dumbfounded –

their long necks, not erect,
their loud honking, still –

this is an enemy
too subtle,
even for them.

2

When the geese honk
they lay their heads down low –
and their long necks roll out –

(Tyrants) (Stupid) (Erect)

As I walk past –
their violence comes.
Honk. Honk. Honk. Honk.

Green Saints on a Tuscan Hillside

Saint Margherita,
iller-looking than Saint Marco
lies with her dusty face
and green skin,

her forehead's skull whitening,
hands nut-withered,
nails, dark and hard
like polished wood.

One foot is green.
The other, black.

I cannot fathom her significance.

Our Book

Our strange, unheard of little book
sought to weld and to betray perhaps in
equal measure. Mad triangle we were.
Three witches in Putney, witches
in love, witches in distrust. Mad I say
we were, musing over our
cauldron Sundays, spinning
talk out of thin air, spinning
love out of hate, real people out of
dreams and dream people from
just sitting there. Who were we?
How many of us were there?
Mad witches we were, spinning love,
spinning distrust, out of thin air.

Mozambique Floods

You'll think I don't think about the
flood. You'll think I don't fear
completely that the water has wet your
smallest toe. I do. I think to call,
to email, send psychic messages
to you; such energy, as ever
wells over into lines which pose as poetry.
I do. I do. I do, but can no
longer. You don't want me to. Not now.
Maybe later, though as I write that I
have neither hope nor, I think, any longer,
desire for such a thing. I only know I
think of your small toes in the flood
and hope they're looking after you –
whilst I also hope you stew. Stew. Stew.

I do.

Upright in Meditation

There was magic in your spine.
Up close I could see it was rigid with fear,
but I did kiss that back I had grown to desire,
and it was you. And you were someone new.

You love me as the sea loves that

You love me as the sea loves that
flatfish and the shark, all about,
over and round – always calm, deep down.

I love, love you as the shark must
love the sea: jagged-toothed,
vicious, with no cause, inside of you.

Porlock

To take in that sweep of sea, is to see it
without eyes.
It was our coast.

Before you there was no sea.
No coast.
No house.
No green.
No horse.
No church.
No scene.

No Wendy pouring translucent
gin and tonic,
giggling like lemonade;
no morning broken
in the stone-grey village
when she died.

The way the car swerved –
there was no view but hedgerows
then, suddenly, the sea.

A short route past car park,
pub and shop,
then house;
the last against extremity.

Just like you and me.
No view but onwards
notwithstanding –
then, suddenly,
all blown out to sea.

You pulled up anchor long ago.
Your mind a message with no bottle.

I knew and didn't know.

The Sun is Setting in the West

The sun is setting in the west;
your house, spot-lit, until the last.

An evening light cracks over Exmoor
lime, to blend with gorse-struck hills;
a rugged horse has made its way
for us.

I feel heavy with blessing,
caught clear and green in your
strange limelight, now, as ever,
in Porlock Hills.

Melbourne

This city sicks up loneliness.
There is you here, eye to eye
with your empty-full flame-leaf
soul, bowing over your drawing
like a cripple drowned in pain,
as the chill, child, sets on the sill.
There is me here, five days from home
and never lonelier. I have half-forgot,
half-formed, half a solid figure
stomping amid ghosts and you,
you are too fucked up to give…
'I have my own pain DO NOT
give me yours.' So I am silent but
I too, now, am empty as hell.

Especially here, here where
wide streets see cars never touch,
never even nearly touch – a land of
paranoia and stupidity. My strength
withers. Where should I be?
Whom do I love? Oh God. Oh God –
and where does he come into all of this?

Planet closing in

Planet closing in,
people, shifting and
who, more or which,
most or when, why –
goodbye. Who cares.
New world, the end.
All false, all gone,
all dreamt, all spent.
Thank God, airport;
London, home, mum,
brother, lover.
Old streets, known streets,
dull streets, small streets.
End, end, end, pain.
Dread, dread, sunshine;
Bali, Middlemarch.
Home, home, home, home.
Mother writes
matchbox England,
England gorgeous –

Goodbye red gum.
Welcome home.
Dread. Dread. Dread. Dread.

Bits and Pieces

A bench, a bank, the smell of apple tree.
Could I feel you near me?

I tracked down the magnetism
of the apple-tree bower, my prism.

Snowdrops I know you too have seen.
Do I hunt you down, like a primal scene?

Again I find your ghost.
Who is it I love most?

Spontaneity
will always bring you back to me.

The cynical, unhappy pause
clogs up the pores.

Do I track you down through country houses
and through your imagined spouses?

Do I intrude
or interlude?

(I never meant it to be rude.)

I hunt you in the wind because
there must be other ways,
if we're to end our magic days.

I see us in the garden.
The garden where we might have been.
The scene we never will have seen.

The magnet of the apple tree
will never bring you home to me.

It is my inspiration
to explore three-sixty degrees of separation.

Is this fear of separating, or love of reality,
to hunt you in the apple tree?

When we've succumbed to sad reality
I'll find you in the apple tree.

It seems I cannot take you with me
so I'll smell you in the apple tree.

Death (days after)

So afraid of death.
Why should we not be –
how could we not be –
seeing as he's on the prowl?

Last night my mother slept with her father's ashes
and our sad animal had crept in with her to die
and she had, tear-stained, come to me and wailed noiselessly
and I had been silent in the face of such things.

It had been easy to forget him,
like gazelle and all the desert deer
caught up in their games and light dances
so that they imagine all the world
to be as bright a dance as theirs –

Ah. How easy
not to scan past those bushes and
their perimeter where he,
their tiger
lurks and lurks.
On days that greet a yellower sky, he
breaks sometimes from deep-down earth,
clasps, and claws and claims
amid screams.

Days after the skies remain yellowish –
the dance of the graceful, rhythmless –
every movement is streaked with unease,
and every goodbye, a stark desert tree
as if it were death's ghost that haunted and hunted still,
and not his victim's soul.

And who can tell
(as how can we after such a year)
if the cat still distorts
because he is still near
(and peering and sneering and causing the bushes to sway…)
or because his power's power, or stain
allows the yellow to hang
which, once commanded as a prop, now
lingers –
long after he himself has turned,
gathered up his pride,
and sauntered off?

Where is it We Go?

When we drop away into the 'dark'
where is it we go? I'd like to know.
I'd like to sludge a torchlight through
in welly boots – and
scowl about intrusively, below.

I'd like to hold my darkness up
(and shake it out),
I'd like to see it drop there
(in the harsh sunlight),
I'd like to trap it in the garden
(and go to meet it).

(I'd need large gloves on. I'd need a hunter's hat...)

You know. I'd like to beat it.